The Teenage Mutant Hero Turtle Joke Book

D1350116

Happy Birthday
Darren, from
Derrick, Catherine
Derrick &
Gary.
xxxx

(Nov. '90)

Other Teenage Mutant Hero Turtle Books
published by Carnival

In the mini hardback series:
Enter: The Rat King
Follow My Leader
Return of the Technodrome
Splinter No More

TEENAGE MUTANT HERO TURTLES™

JOKE BOOK

PETER ELDIN

CARNIVAL

Carnival
An imprint of the Children's Division,
of the Collins Publishing Group,
8 Grafton Street, London W1X 3LA

Published by Carnival 1990

ISBN 0 00 192405 2

Printed and bound in Great Britain by
William Collins Sons & Co. Ltd, Glasgow

Set in Plantin

What do you get if you make fun of a Teenage
    Mutant Hero who is in hot water?
Mock Turtle soup.

What did Hamoto Yoshi say when he was exposed
    to the mutagen?
Don't look now, I'm changing.

What's the difference between Bebop and a flea?
Bebop can have fleas but fleas cannot have Bebops.

When does Rocksteady get jealous of Bebop?
When he hogs the action.

LEONARDO: I want a pizza with two-handed cheese on it.

PIZZA MAN: Two-handed cheese? Why is it called that?

LEONARDO: Because you eat it with one hand and hold your nose with the other.

Which political party do the Turtles support?
The Green Party.

How can you drop a pizza ten feet without breaking it?

Drop it eleven feet and it will remain intact for the first ten feet.

MICHAELANGELO: Hey, you guys. It says in this newspaper that a pizza baker has produced a half hundredweight pizza.

LEONARDO: I don't believe it.

MICHAELANGELO: I knew you'd never swallow that!

What's the difference between Krang and a pizza?
Krang isn't covered with tomato paste.

RAPHAEL: I hear there was trouble at the Pizza Parlour yesterday.
DONATELLO: Yeah – two stale pizzas tried to get fresh.

SHREDDER: How on earth do you manage to make so many mistakes in one day?
BEBOP: I get up early.

What is Bebop's favourite ballet?
Swine Lake.

DONATELLO: What is the definition of hogwash?
LEONARDO: Bebop's laundry!

Why do you call Rocksteady when he's got cotton
  wool in his ears?
Anything you like, because he can't hear you.

SPLINTER: Why are you puffing so much?
LEONARDO: I've just run up the street to stop a
  fight.
SPLINTER: That was noble of you. Who was
  fighting?
LEONARDO: Me and Rocksteady.

ROCKSTEADY: Why do I keep going around in circles?

SHREDDER: Shut up, or I'll nail your other foot to the floor.

SPLINTER: How did Shredder escape from the building? I asked you to watch all exits.

DONATELLO: We did watch all exits. Unfortunately he got out through one of the entrances.

LEONARDO: You must have very clean kitchens in your pizza parlour.

PIZZA MAN: Thank you very much. How can you tell?

LEONARDO: All your pizzas taste of soap.

What is worse than Splinter with a sore nose?
A Turtle with claustrophobia!

SHREDDER: What are you working on now?
BAXTER STOCKMAN: It's a cross between a sheep and a porcupine.
SHREDDER: What does it do?
BAXTER STOCKMAN: It knits its own jumpers.

Do Teenage Mutant Heroes have good memories?
Yes, they have Turtle recall!

LEONARDO: Michaelangelo drove the Turtle Van into the river last night.

SPLINTER: Why did he do that?

LEONARDO: He wanted to dip the headlights.

What's the difference between a Turtle and a chicken?

A Turtle can catch chicken pox but a chicken cannot catch turtle pox.

RAPHAEL: Should pizza be eaten with your fingers?

DONATELLO: No, you should eat your fingers separately.

What would you call a Turtle Roman emperor?
Nero in a Half-Shell.

How would you describe a Happy Hour reporter
  taking a bath?
An April shower.

RAPHAEL: Do you know what pirates used to eat?
LEONARDO: Of course. Pizzas of ate.

Who is the Turtles' favourite poet?
Percy Byshe Shell-ey.

What famous inventor looks after a herd of cows?
Baxter Stock-man.

What did Leonardo say when he saw Bebop wearing dark glasses?
Nothing – he didn't recognize him!

What would you call Rocksteady when he complains?
A whine-oceros.

Why did Michaelangelo climb on to the roof of the pizza parlour?
Because the waiter said that the pizzas were on the house.

BAXTER STOCKMAN: I've just invented a pill that's half glue and half aspirin.
SHREDDER: What's it for?
BAXTER STOCKMAN: It's for people with splitting headaches.

How did the man kill himself in the Turtles'
   headquarters?
He committed sewer-cide.

What's the difference between Rocksteady, the rhino, and a loaf of bread?
I don't know.
Well, if you don't know, I'm not going to send you shopping!

LEONARDO: Would you like to come to a party tomorrow, April?
APRIL: I'm sorry, Leonardo. I can't come. I'm going to see Romeo and Juliet.
LEONARDO: Well, bring them, too. We'll have a great time.

Why did Rocksteady jump from the top of the Post Office Tower?
He wanted to be a big hit in London.

MICHAELANGELO: I'd like some Mexican chilli on my pizza, please.
PIZZA MAN: How do you make a Mexican chilli?
MICHAELANGELO: Put ice cubes down his trousers.

LEONARDO: Why aren't you eating your pizza?
RAPHAEL: I'm waiting for the mustard to cool down.

WHO GAVE YOU THAT BLACK EYE?

NO-ONE GAVE IT TO ME. I HAD TO FIGHT FOR IT.

ROCKSTEADY: Shredder! Bebop is going out.
SHREDDER: I didn't know he was on fire!

What would you call Teenage Mutant Turtles who are worth nothing?
Zeroes in a Half-Shell.

DONATELLO: Rocksteady and Bebop will not harm you if you carry your stick.
SPLINTER: Perhaps – it probably depends upon how fast I carry it.

ROCKSTEADY: When were you born?
BEBOP: Second of April.
ROCKSTEADY: Oh, a day too late.

What do the Turtles say when they part company?
We shell meet again.

The Turtles, Splinter, April and Irma were shelter-
ing under one umbrella but none of them got
wet. Why?
It wasn't raining.

This is April O'Neil with the Happy Hour news.
Early today someone punched a hole in the fence
surrounding the local nudist camp. Police are looking into it.

ROCKSTEADY: Can I tell you a joke about quicksand?
BEBOP: Is it good?
ROCKSTEADY: Yes, but it will take some time to sink
in.

What did Michaelangelo say to April O'Neil after
she'd spent four days in a beehive?
Hi honey!

BEBOP: That's a nasty wound you've got on your forehead. How did you get it?

ROCKSTEADY: I bit myself.

BEBOP: How on earth could you bite yourself on the forehead?

ROCKSTEADY: I stood on a chair.

Why is Bebop unpopular?
Because he's such a boar.

What is as big as Krang's robot body but doesn't
  weigh anything?
Its shadow.

DONATELLO: I've been reading a book on body building and I've been doing the exercises in it for two months.

MICHAELANGELO: Has it done you any good?

DONATELLO: I should say so! I can now lift the book above my head!

ROCKSTEADY: Why are you driving that steamroller over your potato field?
BEBOP: I want to grow mashed potatoes.

PIZZA MAN: Would you like some more of my special pizza?
MICHAELANGELO: No, thanks. I'm too young to die.

What is Krang's favourite song?
Fangs for the memory.

Why did Bebop sprinkle sugar all over his pillow?
He wanted to have sweet dreams.

DONATELLO: I'll have a pizza, please.
PIZZA MAN: With pleasure.
DONATELLO: No, with mozzarella.

What did the pizza say to the tomato?
That's enough of your sauce!

Rocksteady and Bebop are arranging to meet near the Technodrome. 'If I get there first I'll put a chalk mark on the door, said Rocksteady.

'Good idea,' said Bebop. 'And if I get there first I'll rub it off.'

What did the doughnut say to the pizza?

If I had as much dough as you, I wouldn't be hanging around this hole.

KRANG: What invention is Baxter Stockman working on now?
SHREDDER: He's trying to cross a hyena and a parrot.
KRANG: What for?
SHREDDER: He hopes to develop an animal that laughs at its own jokes.

LEONARDO: Will the pizzas be long?
PIZZA MAN: No, sir. They'll be round.

DONATELLO: I love pizzas.
LEONARDO: So do I, but I prefer candles.
DONATELLO: Candles? Why candles?
LEONARDO: Because I'm into light meals.

SHREDDER: What are you working on now professor?

BAXTER STOCKMAN: I have just invented a universal solvent, a liquid that dissolves anything it touches.

SHREDDER: That sounds great. Are there any problems?

BAXTER STOCKMAN: Yes, just one. It dissolves everything it touches – so what do I keep it in?

One day there was a knock at the door of the Technodrome and Rocksteady went to answer it.

When he came back Shredder asked, 'Who was that at the door?'

'It was a tramp,' replied Rocksteady. 'He said he hadn't had a bite for weeks – so I bit him!'

BEBOP: How did you get all those bruises?

ROCKSTEADY: I started to go through a revolving door and then changed my mind.

Why did Raphael drive the Turtle Van in reverse?
Because he knows the Highway Code backwards.

What's the difference between Turtles and soldiers?
You can't dip Turtles in your egg.

What's the difference between Rocksteady when he
is ill and a dead bee?
*Rocksteady when ill is a seedy beast, and a dead bee is
a bee deceased.*

Why did Bebop put his watch in the bank?
He was trying to save time.

SPLINTER: I'm going to get up at dawn tomorrow to watch the sunrise.
LEONARDO: If you'd picked a better time I would have come with you.

What did Splinter think when the Shredder caught him by the tail?
That's the end of me.

ROCKSTEADY: Why have you got your head on that grinding wheel?
BEBOP: I'm trying to sharpen my wits.

What's the difference between the Technodrome and Joan of Arc?
One is made of metal; the other is Maid of Orleans.

What petrol do the Turtles use in their Turtle Van?
Shell.

If Splinter lost his tail where would he go for a new one?
To the re-tailer.

What looks like a plum but always comes to the rescue?
A Greengage Mutant Hero Turtle.

What is the Turtles' least favourite breakfast cereal?
Shredder Wheat.

What ant cannot talk?
A mute-ant.

RAPHAEL: What's the difference between Rocksteady and a matterbaby?
LEONARDO: What's a matterbaby?
RAPHAEL: Nothing, but it was kind of you to ask.

MICHAELANGELO: Master Splinter, why do you often talk to yourself?

SPLINTER: Because I like to talk to an intelligent person, and I like to hear intelligent answers.

What's the difference between a biscuit and Rocksteady?

You can dunk a biscuit in your tea.

LEONARDO: Hey! There's a cockroach on my pizza!

PIZZA MAN: Oh yes. The little devils will eat anything.

BEBOP: Rocksteady doesn't know the meaning of the word 'fear'.

SHREDDER: That's because he's too afraid to ask.

RAPHAEL: I don't think much of this pizza.

PIZZA MAN: I'll have you know that I was making pizzas before you were born.

RAPHAEL: Yes, I think that was one of them!

What do you get if you cross a Teenage Mutant Hero with a pigeon?

A Turtledove.

BAXTER STOCKMAN: I've just crossed an owl with a skunk.

SHREDDER: What did you get.

BAXTER STOCKMAN: A bird that smells but doesn't give a hoot.

ROCKSTEADY to BEBOP: I do wish you wouldn't eat with your fingers. Why don't you use the shovel like I taught you?

41

What's the difference between a hungry Turtle and
a greedy Turtle?
One longs to eat and the other eats too long.

LEONARDO: Why do you call Bebop 'Isaiah'?
RAPHAEL: Because one eye's higher than the other.

Why did Bebop lie down in the fireplace?
He wanted to sleep like a log.

BEBOP: I think I'm losing my memory.
ROCKSTEADY: What makes you say that?
BEBOP: What makes me say what?

BEBOP: Why are you carrying a compass?
ROCKSTEADY: So I know whether I'm coming or going.

MICHAELANGELO: What have I got in my hands?
DONATELLO: A three-storey building.
MICHAELANGELO: You peeped!

Why did April O'Neil put a torch in her mouth?
She was trying to get an inside story.

BAXTER STOCKMAN: I've just crossed a hyena with a gorilla.
SHREDDER: What did you get?
BAXTER STOCKMAN: I don't know. But you'd better laugh when it does!

If one of the Shredder's foot soldiers crossed the road, fell in some mud and then came back again, what would you call him?
A dirty double crosser.

What's Rocksteady's favourite river in Germany?
The River Rhine-o.

What looks exactly the same as half a pizza?
The other half.

BEBOP: How long can someone live without a brain?
ROCKSTEADY: I don't know. How old are you?

Why are spinning tops like the Turtles?
Because they are always doing good turns.

What is the Turtles' favourite place in Italy?
The Leaning Tower of Pizza.

SHREDDER: You'd make a good dancer, except for two things.
ROCKSTEADY: What?
SHREDDER: Your feet.

What is green, has a shell and wears dark glasses?
A Teenage Mutant Hero Turtle in disguise.

What do you call Teenage Mutant Turtles who stink?
Heroes who don't half smell!

SHREDDER: You are always complaining, Krang. You are like a bird.
KRANG: Like a bird? What do you mean?
SHREDDER: You're a grouse.

How do you stop Krang's Rock Soldiers from charging?
Take away their credit cards.

RAPHAEL: Why aren't you talking to me?

LEONARDO: Because you are not here.

RAPHAEL: Of course I'm here.

LEONARDO: No you're not, and I can prove it.

RAPHAEL: Go on, then.

LEONARDO: Well, you're not in London are you?

RAPHAEL: No.

LEONARDO: Are you in New York?

RAPHAEL: No.

LEONARDO: Well, if you're not in London and you're not in New York, you must be somewhere else. Right?

RAPHAEL: Right.

LEONARDO: Well, if you're somewhere else, you're not here!

As he walked out of the pizza parlour Michaelangelo handed the cashier a piece of paper. On the paper was written the numbers 1004180.

A few days later the cashier asked Michaelangelo what the note meant.

'Well,' explained Michaelangelo, 'on that day I didn't order anything did I?'

The cashier agreed.

Michaelangelo then read out the meaning of the numbers 1004180 he had written on the slip. 'I owe nothing for I ate nothing.'

What happened when Bebop went to a mind reader?
She gave him his money back.

Shredder ordered his two henchmen to attack the Turtles. Bebop went into the fray with his fists flailing violently but did not manage to hit any of the Turtles.

'Have I caused the Turtles any damage?' he shouted to Shredder.

'No,' Shredder replied. 'But keep those fists flying – the draught may give them a cold.'

What's the difference between a Turtle who has signed a legal document and a Turtle who has eaten several pizzas?
One has signed and dated, the other is dined and sated.

DONATELLO: What is the Italian for a slice of pizza?
MICHAELANGELO: I've no idea.
DONATELLO: A pizza pizza.

What do you get if you wrap a warm scarf around the neck of a Teenage Mutant Hero?
A Turtle neck sweater.

BAXTER STOCKMAN: Hey! I've just worked out how to get all the Turtles in a matchbox.
SHREDDER: How on earth can you do that?
BAXTER STOCKMAN: The big secret is to take the matches out first.

Michaelangelo asked the pizza man what toppings he had. The pizza man whispered hoarsely, 'Pepperoni, tuna, four seasons, mozzarella, tomato. . .'

Michaelangelo was concerned by the man's hoarseness so he asked, 'Do you have laryngitis?'

'No,' said the pizza man. 'Just pepperoni, tuna, four seasons, mozzarella, tomato . . .'

Who stands on one leg, flies and invents things?
Baxter Storkman.

What are green, do good deeds, have shells and are rather windy?
Teenage Mutant Hero Burples.

Why did Bebop throw his alarm clock out of the
   window?
He wanted to kill time.

ROCKSTEADY: Why are you standing on your head?
BEBOP: I'm just turning things over in my mind.

Why is a Turtle adventurous?
He's not afraid to stick his neck out.

What meat do Turtles like?
Donatello kebabs.

BEBOP: Can you lend me 10c to call a friend?
ROCKSTEADY: Here's 20c – call all of them.

The Turtles were approaching the Technodrome when a horrible monster from Dimension X appeared. 'Don't panic,' said Michaelangelo. 'Remember what the book says. If faced with a monster from Dimension X simply stand still and it will go away.'

'Groovy idea, man,' said Donatello. 'You've read the book and I've read the book, but has the monster read the book?'

What would you call funny Teenage Mutant Turtles?
Heroes in a Laugh-Shell.

KRANG: What crazy invention has Baxter Stockman come up with this time?
SHREDDER: Non-stick glue.

Who is Rocksteady's favourite composer?
Tuskanini.

KRANG: Why is Baxter Stockman shaking?
SHREDDER: It's his latest invention, a cross between a sheep dog and a jelly.
KRANG: Why should that make him shake?
SHREDDER: He's got the collie wobbles.

MICHAELANGELO: Master Splinter, where were you born?
SPLINTER: Japan.
MICHAELANGELO: What part?
SPLINTER: All of me.

What do you call an acrobatic Teenage Mutant Hero?
A topsy turvy Turtle.

The Turtles were carrying out a heroic deed in a multi-storey skyscraper. Unfortunately the criminal they were chasing managed to get away and set fire to the building.

Leonardo and Michaelangelo were trapped by the inferno.

Michaelangelo said, 'Quick, let's jump out of the window.'

'But we're on the thirteenth floor!' protested Leonardo.

As the flames licked around them Michaelangelo replied, 'Jump! This is no time to get superstitious.'

What's the best way to attract the attention of the Turtles?
Make a noise like a pizza.

Why are pizza bakers silly?
Because they sell what they knead.

Why is Krang musical?
He has sharp teeth.

What steps would you take if you come face to face
with Shredder?
Very big ones!

Did you hear about the pizza baker who was so
weak that when he tried to beat some eggs, the
eggs won?

RAPHAEL: What's the best thing to put in a pizza?
MICHAELANGELO: Your teeth.

How do you tell if Krang's robot body is in your
   fridge?
The door will not shut.

This April O'Neil with the Happy Hour News on
Channel Six. Osbert Pennyfickle, Member of Par-
liament for Twiddlewich, took his seat in the House
of Commons yesterday. Today he was made to take
it back.

Hi, this is April O'Neil presenting the Happy Hour News on Channel Six. Early today two men broke into the home of Mr and Mrs Hirenbacker. A distressed Mrs Hirenbacker told me that the burglars took everything except the soap and towels. Police are now searching for the dirty crooks.

Why did Shredder take a bath when the Turtles attacked the Technodrome?
He wanted to make a clean getaway.

MICHAELANGELO: Waiter, do you have any wild duck?
WAITER: No, sir. But I can get a tame one and annoy it for you.

BEBOP: I got an anonymous letter today.
ROCKSTEADY: Really? Who was it from?

Which side of a pizza is the left side?
The side that hasn't been eaten.

This is April O'Neil with the Happy Hour News. The tug-of-war between France and England has been cancelled. No-one could find a rope long enough to go across the Channel.

BAXTER STOCKMAN: Don't disturb me, Shredder. I'm working on my latest invention.
SHREDDER: What's that?
BAXTER STOCKMAN: A waterproof tea-bag.

ROCKSTEADY: Why are you scratching yourself?
BEBOP: No one else knows where I itch.

Why should you never scratch a rat?
You might get a Splinter in your finger.

Why is Splinter a poor dancer?
Because he has two left feet.

Why did Michaelangelo eat his pizza quickly?
He wanted to finish it before he lost his appetite.

ROCKSTEADY: What are you doing?
BEBOP: I'm writing a letter to myself.
ROCKSTEADY: What does it say?
BEBOP: I won't know until I get it tomorrow.

KRANG: What happened to that waterproof, shock-proof, anti-magnetic, unbreakable watch I gave you?
SHREDDER: I lost it.

Why does the baker make pizzas for the Turtles?
He does it for the dough.

Why are pizzas polite?
Because they are always well bread.

BEBOP: I've changed my mind.
ROCKSTEADY: Good. I hope the new one is better than the old one.

RAPHAEL: I was surrounded by lots of lions this
   morning.
LEONARDO: Were you scared?
RAPHAEL: Of course not – they were dandelions.

SPLINTER: Robbers have stolen the world's biggest store of prunes.
LEONARDO: Do you think we could catch them?
SPLINTER: You should be able to – they're still on the run.

RAPHAEL: Have you lived in these sewers all your life, Master Splinter?
SPLINTER: Not yet.

RAPHAEL: If I paid twenty cents for four pizzas what would each one be?
DONATELLO: Stale!

Why did Bebop go to an audition for a seafaring film dressed as a tree?
He wanted to be the captain's log.

What did the grape say when Rocksteady stood on it?
Nothing, it just gave out a little whine.

RAPHAEL: How do you make a Swiss Roll?
LEONARDO: Push him over the Alps.

If Shredder has something special to tell Krang,
how does he talk to him?
Face to stomach.

What would get if you crossed Rocksteady with a
horse?
A rhine-horse-eros.

MICHAELANGELO: What is worse than a centipede
with corns?
DONATELLO: I don't know.
MICHAELANGELO: Krang with toothache!

Would you rather Krang attacked you, or the
Shredder?
I'd rather he attacked the Shredder.

What do you do if you go out for a meal with
Krang?
Give him the biggest serving.

RAPHAEL: I've bought you a present, Donatello, your favourite pizza – pepperoni with peanut butter and treacle!

DONATELLO: But there are only a few crumbs in this box.

RAPHAEL: It's my favourite, too!

What would you do if you saw Shredder, Rocksteady and Bebop walking along the street?

I'd hope they were three ordinary people going to a fancy dress party.

LEONARDO: You've only got one type of pizza on the menu, but you told me there would be a choice.

PIZZA MAN: There is a choice – you can either take it or leave it.

ROCKSTEADY: How do you keep an idiot in suspense?

BEBOP: How?

ROCKSTEADY: I'll tell you next week.

BEBOP: I think I'm losing my mind.

ROCKSTEADY: Don't worry. You won't miss it.

RAPHAEL: There's a dead fly on my pizza.

PIZZA MAN: Yes, sir, it's the heat that kills them.

What do you get if you cross Krang with a rose?
I don't know, but I wouldn't try smelling it.

Why was Bebop unsuccessful on Krang's oil rigs?
He kept throwing bread to the helicopters.

Why doesn't Krang do anything daring?
Because he hasn't got any guts.

Why does Krang file his teeth?
He eats a lot of tinned fruit.

RAPHAEL: I'm glad you named me Raphael, Master Splinter.

SPLINTER: Why is that?

RAPHAEL: Because that is what the other Turtles call me.

SPLINTER: Why is Leonardo looking so miserable?

RAPHAEL: Because I wouldn't give him a piece of my pizza.

SPLINTER: Has his all gone?

RAPHAEL: Yes, and he wasn't very happy when I ate that either.

DONATELLO: What is your favourite nut?
RAPHAEL: Cashew.
DONATELLO: Bless you!

MICHAELANGELO: Every night I dream that Bebop and Rocksteady are hiding under my bed. What can I do?
DONATELLO: Saw the legs off your bed.

SHREDDER: I'd like some rat poison.

CHEMIST: Sorry, sir. We don't stock it. Have you tried Boots?

SHREDDER: Look – I want to poison Splinter, not kick him!

What would you get if you crossed Bebop with a python?

A crushing bore.

What did the river say when Rocksteady sat in it?
Well, I'll be dammed!

What's the difference between a thunderstorm and
    Krang with toothache?
One pours with rain, the other roars with pain.

Why does Bebop put hay under his pillow at night?
To feed his night-mares.

What's the difference between a comma and
    Splinter?
*A comma is a pause at the end of a clause, and Splinter
has claws at the end of his paws.*

Did you hear that Krang's ambition is to be an
    actor?
He is looking for a part he can get his teeth into.

BAXTER STOCKMAN: I've invented a new way of creating baked apples.

SHREDDER: What's that?

BAXTER STOCKMAN: I set fire to the orchard.

DONATELLO: What musical instrument goes with pizza?

LEONARDO: I've no idea. What musical instrument goes with pizza?

DONATELLO: Pickle-o

Bebop was in the kitchen of the Technodrome hitting the milk bottles with a piece of rope.

Rocksteady walked in and said, 'What are you doing that for?'

Bebop replied, 'I'm making whipped cream.'

APRIL: I was really proud of you when you dived from that skyscraper into the river to rescue that lady who was drowning.

RAPHAEL: Thanks, April. What I want to know is, who pushed me?

What's the difference between Krang and peanut
   butter?
Krang doesn't get stuck to the roof of your mouth.

RAPHAEL: Why did you wake me up? It's still dark.
LEONARDO: Try opening your eyes.

What does Krang write on his Christmas cards?
Best vicious of the season.

When is Rocksteady like a camera?
When he snaps.

Where does Bebop keep his money?
In a piggy bank.

What do you get if you cross a Turtle with a boy
scout?
A Turtle that helps old ladies cross the road.

Why does Rocksteady have a bell on his bicycle?
Because his horn doesn't work.

ROCKSTEADY: Can you stand on your head?
BEBOP: No, it's too high.

What's the best way to talk to Krang?
Over the 'phone.

The Turtles were chasing a crook through a supermarket but they lost him. He jumped on a scale and got a weigh.

Here is the Happy Hour News from April O'Neil. Yesterday the well-known Scottish wardrobe assistant, Angus McCoatup, washed his kilt. Now he can't do a fling with it.

SHREDDER: Why are you so angry?
KRANG: Because it's all the rage.

Leonardo was in the pizza parlour. He went up to the counter to buy a drink and when he returned to his table there was a big, ugly man sitting in his place.

'Excuse me, sir,' said Leonardo, 'you're sitting on my seat.'

'Prove it,' snarled the ugly man.

'That's easy,' replied Leonardo. 'You're sitting on my pizza.'

LEONARDO: Please can I have a pepperoni pizza without olives?

PIZZA MAN: I'm sorry, we're out of olives. Will you have it without anchovies?

Why didn't Krang go to the ball?
He had no body to go with.

BAXTER STOCKMAN: I'm trying to cross an octopus
 with a cow.
SHREDDER: What for?
BAXTER STOCKMAN: I'm hoping to get an animal that
 will milk itself.

THIS IS APRIL O'NEIL WITH A NEWS FLASH FROM CHANNEL SIX. A GHOST HAS JUST BEEN GIVEN A JOB IN THE HOUSE OF COMMONS. HE IS GOING TO BE THE SPOOKER OF THE HOUSE.

Dad, come quickly! Mum's fighting Krang and
 Shredder!
*Don't worry about it, Son. I'm sure Krang and
 Shredder can look after themselves!*

LEONARDO: Did you manage to mend my Turtle-
Com, Donatello?
DONATELLO: It isn't broken, Leonardo. The battery
is flat.
LEONARDO: What shape should it be?

How can you stop pizzas getting stale?
Eat them.

What did Bebop do when Rocksteady told him there was a flea in his ear?
He shot it.

Who has the most dangerous job in the Technodrome?
Krang's dentist!

Why is Splinter sitting on a wall like a coin?
Because he has a head on one side and a tail on the other.

What would you call Bebop when he drives a car?
A road hog.

This is April O'Neil with the Happy Hour News. Workers in the Royal Mint are threatening to go on strike. They want to make less money.

What's the difference between potatoes and the Turtles?
You can't mash Turtles.

LEONARDO: Hasn't Splinter got a long nose!

MICHAELANGELO: Yes, during the winter he puts snow on it and lets it out as a ski resort.

APRIL: I'd like you guys to take Irma to the zoo.

TURTLES: No way. It they want her they'll have to come and get her.

When is a cowardly Shredder like a Teenage
   Mutant Hero?
When he turns Turtle and runs.

What did Rocksteady say into the microphone?
Tusking, tusking . . . one, two, three . . . tusking.

BEBOP: I've got something preying on my mind.
ROCKSTEADY: Don't worry. It'll soon die of starvation.

What does a Turtle suffer with if you frighten him?
Shell shock.

Why did April and Irma walk over the hill?
Because they couldn't walk under it.

SHREDDER: Why did you stop working on your time machine?

BAXTER STOCKMAN: I decided there was no future in it.

Why are the Turtles mean with money?
They don't like to shell out.

What moves when it's not fast and doesn't move
when it's fast?
The Turtles' Blimp.

What's Krang's favourite breakfast?
Dimension X and bacon.

DROWNING MAN: Help! Help! I can't swim.
ROCKSTEADY: So what? I can't play the piano but I
don't go around shouting about it.

DONATELLO: I keep dreaming of kangaroos.
SPLINTER: Don't worry. They're only hoptical
illusions.